SLIP STREAM GRAPHICS

BEYOND THE
WALL

JONNY ZUCKER AND TOMAS ARANDA

EDGE FRANKLIN WATTS

LONDON·SYDNEY

BEYOND THE
WALL

On one side of the 'wall' a girl called
Zara lives in Ark City.

On the other side of the 'wall' a boy
called Kell lives in Grey City.

No one from the two cities has ever
met before. Until now...

First published in 2014 by
Franklin Watts
338 Euston Road
London NW1 3BH

Franklin Watts Australia
Level 17/207 Kent Street
Sydney, NSW 2000

Text © Jonny Zucker 2014
Illustrations © Franklin Watts 2014

A CIP catalogue record for this book
is available from the British Library.

ISBN (pb): 978 1 4451 3090 3
ISBN (Library ebook): 978 1 4451 3096 5

Series Editors: Adrian Cole and Jackie Hamley
Series Advisors: Diana Bentley and Dee Reid
Series Designer: Peter Scoulding

A paperback original

1 3 5 7 9 10 8 6 4 2

Printed in China

Franklin Watts is a division of
Hachette Children's Books,
an Hachette UK company
www.hachette.co.uk

In Grey City...

Zara's house, Ark City.

Father, I must talk to you. There is a city on the other side—

Stub! I didn't know *you* were here.

8

Later...

I must help them!

I can't believe we pump our waste into their city...

Stub has been lying to all of us.

These are the people who power our city.

We must free them all!

SLIP STREAM

Slipstream is a series of expertly levelled books designed for pupils who are struggling with reading. Its unique three-strand approach through fiction, graphic fiction and non-fiction gives pupils a rich reading experience that will accelerate their progress and close the reading gap.

At the heart of every Slipstream graphic fiction book is a great story. Easily accessible words and phrases ensure that pupils both decode and comprehend, and the high interest stories really engage older struggling readers.

Whether you're using Slipstream Level 2 for Guided Reading or as an independent read, here are some suggestions:

1. Make each reading session successful. Talk about the text or pictures before the pupil starts reading. Introduce any unfamiliar vocabulary.

2. Encourage the pupil to talk about the book using a range of open questions. For example, what would they do if waste from their home was being pumped into another city? What do they think should happen to Stub?

3. Discuss the differences between reading fiction, graphic fiction and non-fiction. Which do they prefer?

For guidance, SLIPSTREAM Level 2 – Beyond The Wall has been approximately measured to:

National Curriculum Level: 2b
Reading Age: 7.6–8.0
Book Band: Purple

ATOS: 2.0*
Guided Reading Level: I
Lexile® Measure (confirmed): 250L

*Please check actual Accelerated Reader™ book level and quiz availability at www.arbookfind.co.uk